Science Fair Winners

EXPERIMENTS TO DO ON YOUR
FAMILY

20 projects and experiments about sisters,
brothers, parents, pets, and the rest of the gang

by Karen Romano Young

Illustrations by David Goldin

NATIONAL GEOGRAPHIC

WASHINGTON, D.C.

credits

PUBLISHED BY THE NATIONAL GEOGRAPHIC SOCIETY

John M. Fahey, Jr., *President and Chief Executive Officer*
Gilbert M. Grosvenor, *Chairman of the Board*
Tim T. Kelly, *President, Global Media Group*
John Q. Griffin, *Executive Vice President; President, Publishing*
Nina D. Hoffman, *Executive Vice President; President, Book Publishing Group*
Melina Gerosa Bellows, *Executive Vice President, Children's Publishing*

PREPARED BY THE BOOK DIVISION

Nancy Laties Feresten, *Vice President, Editor in Chief, Children's Books*
Jonathan Halling, *Director of Design, Children's Publishing*
Jennifer Emmett, *Executive Editor, Children's Books*
Carl Mehler, *Director of Maps*
R. Gary Colbert, *Production Director*
Jennifer A. Thornton, *Managing Editor*

STAFF FOR THIS BOOK

Priyanka Lamichhane, *Editor*
James Hiscott, Jr., *Art Director / Designer*
Grace Hill, *Associate Managing Editor*
Lewis R. Bassford, *Production Manager*
Susan Borke, *Legal and Business Affairs*

MANUFACTURING AND QUALITY MANAGEMENT

Christopher A. Liedel, *Chief Financial Officer*
Phillip L. Schlosser, *Vice President*
Chris Brown, *Technical Director*
Nicole Elliott, *Manager*
Rachel Faulise, *Manager*
Robert Barr, *Manager*

ACKNOWLEDGMENTS

Rowan Candy, Infant Vision Laboratory, Indiana University
Preston B. Cline, Wharton Leadership Ventures, University of Pennsylvania
James E. Crowe, Jr.; Terry Dermody; George Hill, Vanderbilt University
Laurie Kramer, University of Illinois at Urbana-Champaign
Julie C. Lumeng, University of Michigan
Julie Mennella, Monell Chemical Senses Center
Daniel I. Rees, University of Colorado at Denver
Nancy L. Segal, Twin Studies Center, California State University, Fullerton
Daniel Shaw, University of Pittsburgh
Barry Starr, Stanford University and The Tech Museum

The National Geographic Society is one of the world's largest nonprofit scientific and educational organizations. Founded in 1888 to "increase and diffuse geographic knowledge," the Society works to inspire people to care about the planet. It reaches more than 325 million people worldwide each month through its official journal, *National Geographic*, and other magazines; National Geographic Channel; television documentaries; music; radio; films; books; DVDs; maps; exhibitions; school publishing programs; interactive media; and merchandise. National Geographic has funded more than 9,000 scientific research, conservation and exploration projects and supports an education program combating geographic illiteracy. For more information, visit nationalgeographic.com.

For more information, please call 1-800-NGS LINE (647-5463) or write to the following address:
National Geographic Society
1145 17th Street N.W.
Washington, D.C. 20036-4688 U.S.A.

Visit us online at www.nationalgeographic.com/books
For librarians and teachers: www.ngchildrensbooks.org
More for kids from National Geographic: kids.nationalgeographic.com

For information about special discounts for bulk purchases, please contact National Geographic Books Special Sales: ngspecsales@ngs.org

For rights or permissions inquiries, please contact National Geographic Books Subsidiary Rights: ngbookrights@ngs.org

Paperback ISBN: 978-1-4263-0691-4
Library binding ISBN: 978-1-4263-0692-1

Many of the projects in this book involve human or animal subjects. The International Science and Engineering Fair (ISEF) rules include specific requirements for these types of projects. Students should familiarize themselves generally with the ISEF rules as well as the rules specific to animal and human subjects. Students also need to complete all necessary documents to ensure their project complies with the ISEF requirements. Students who have questions should seek clarification from their teachers.

You can find additional information on the ISEF website:
www.societyforscience.org/isef/about/index.asp
www.societyforscience.org/Page.aspx?pid=312

Printed in the United States of America
10/WOR/1

THE WORKSHOPS

WELCOME TO FAMILY SCIENCE

the introduction

FAMILY SCIENCE is dedicated to helping you design a science fair project that will wow your teachers and judges—and that grows out of your own interests, passions, and goals.

IMPORTANT: *All research involving human and vertebrate animals is strictly regulated and requires prior review and approval. When you do any science fair project that involves people and other vertebrate animals, you need to make a special application to your science fair committee. Make sure you and your teacher comply with all legal guidelines, including the ISEF rules. Find out the rules ahead of time, and be sure to get the permission you need.*

You'll find the International Science and Engineering Fair rules here: **http://www.societyforscience. org/isef/rulesandguidelines**

Social sciences aren't usually studied until college, so you might wonder whether they are "real" sciences. They sure are. The International Science and Engineering Fair has a whole category called Behavior and Social Science, which competes equally with math, physics, and biology projects. You'll learn to

- ask a question and turn it into a study
- make observations, make comparisons, and draw conclusions (the building blocks of the scientific method), which will lead you to . . .
- do your own research based on the work of scientists who are

doing great projects in the fields of developmental psychology (how people's attitudes develop as they grow), genetics (how shared heredity affects siblings), biopsychology (how people's attitudes relate to upbringing), applied family studies (which involves, among other topics, fighting among siblings), and even energy science (how efficiently your family uses fuel).

which workshop?

Some of these workshops involve experiments and some of them are observations and surveys because scientists use various methods of research. Here's a way to think about the differences:

You **experiment** when you ask a question and devise a way to change a situation and observe what happens.

You **observe** when you notice things and see them as part of interrelated systems.

You **survey** when you gather data from a variety of subjects and use the data to answer a question.

Some of these workshops seem really science-y. Some of them don't. This might be because you define science in terms of nature: biology (the study of life), chemistry (the elements), or physics (time, space, motion, etc). But this book includes workshops that look at families through the social sciences, too. These sciences include psychology (what's in someone's head), sociology (how a group and members of a group behave), anthropology (the study of humans), and educational theory (the study of learning).

Some of the workshops seem hard and some seem easy. This difference might depend on what you find easy to do and what challenges you. It's all good science, though. If you're not sure whether a workshop will satisfy science fair requirements, ask before you get started—*especially* with any project involving people.

What if...? I wonder...?
How can I find out...?

These three questions are the start of all science. They lead to observing, experimenting, reaching a conclusion, and finding another question, which leads you to more science and more watching, testing, and understanding, which leads to another question. . . . Well, you get the idea.

what is family science?

People study many different aspects of family relationships to learn what difference it makes to share genes, parents, rooms, food, and many other things. They've learned that these relationships are linked to what we do, how we grow, and how we relate to the rest of the world.

> "The best scientists are often B students. **Perfectionists have a hard time dealing with failure.** Science is full of dead ends and failures. **Being comfortable with uncertainty** and the fact that things might not work can be the mark of a good scientist."

— Terry Dermody, *Vanderbilt University*

What is a sibling?

A brother or sister. Here are some different kinds of siblings:

- **blood sibling:** related by blood
- **adoptive sibling:** related by adoption
- **full sibling:** brother or sister who shares biological parents OR adoptive parents with you
- **half sibling:** brother or sister who shares one biological parent OR adoptive parent
  - **uterine half sibling:** shares a biological mother with you (different fathers)
  - **agnate or consanguine half sibling:** shares a father with you (different mothers)
- **stepsibling:** brother or sister who shares no biological OR adoptive parents with you
- **twins, triplets, quadruplets, quintuplets, sextuplets:** babies born from the same pregnancy
  - **identical twins:** babies produced from the same egg
  - **fraternal twins:** babies produced from different eggs
  - **virtual twins:** siblings brought into a family in nine months or less through birth and adoption or through two adoptions

Who is studying sibling relationships?

Lots of scientists in Europe, the United States, and Canada are doing research on brothers and sisters. Scientists have long wondered what makes our personalities the way they are: Is it genetics? Is it parents? Is it friends? Some of the questions they're asking involve birth order, diseases and cures, competition, violence, peacemaking skills, ability to negotiate, and relationships with the opposite sex.

Why is studying pets important?

Studying the behavior and biology of other species sheds light on our own. The workshops in this book that involve short-term pet training help you see a pet's process of learning and allow you to compare animal and human abilities.

MEET MY BIG BROTHER
(Determine whether birth order is linked to height)

the basics

MANY PEOPLE, including physicians and psychologists, consider birth order to be a major influence on personality, success, even physical growth. Many firstborns are surgeons and CEOs. Middle children are often mediators or peacekeepers. Youngest children are likely to be artists and adventurers.

TIME NEEDED > two weeks to conduct research and compile results

SCIENCE > statistics, physical development

SCIENCE CONCEPT > finding a correlation between height and birth order

ADULT INVOLVEMENT > In order to find adult siblings to participate, ask adults you know to answer your questionnaire about their birth order and height. Remember to comply with all legal guidelines, including ISEF rules. See the resources section for links.

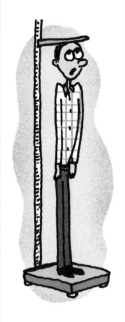

> " While firstborns score especially well on... **conscientiousness**—a sense of general responsibility and follow-through—later-borns score higher on what's known as **agreeableness,** or the simple ability to get along in the world. "

— Jeffrey Kluger,
Time

the buzz

David Lawson of University College in London found that children with three older siblings were 2.5 cm shorter than the average height for their age. As children grew up, older siblings reached or surpassed average height, but younger children remained of below-average height.

the lingo

birth order—a sibling's position in the family

you'll need

Internet access for research on average height per age
e-mail
height measurement tools:
- steel tape measure
- chalk
notebook

the QUESTION >>

Can you observe a relationship between height and birth order?

the PLAN >>

Find and compare the heights and birth orders of subjects to see if a pattern emerges.

what to do

1 **MAKE UP** a questionnaire to send to as many subjects as possible. It should ask their height, age, gender, number of siblings, and place in birth order. Give the following directions for measuring a person's height. Answers should be anonymous. Also measure yourself. If you're measuring someone in person, here's how to be most accurate:

A. Have the subject stand with his or her heels against a wall. Draw a chalk line at the level of the top of the subject's head.

B. Have the subject step away.

C. Measure from the floor to the line you drew. To be truly scientific, use metric measurement.

2 **USE A WEBSITE** [see workshop resources] or an almanac to learn the average height for each age group you find in your answers. Note that men and women have different average heights, so separate your subjects accordingly. And the charts sometimes separate races and ethnicities. Calculate the difference between each subject's height and the average height by dividing the subject's height by the average height. The answer will be a positive or negative percentage. For example, your subject is a 48-year-old African-American woman, an oldest child, with a height of 5´9˝, or 175.26 cm. The average height of a 48-year-old African-American woman is 164 cm. So your subject is 106.87% above average height,

11.26 cm above average. Make this calculation for each of your subjects.

3 **GATHER DATA** into groups by birth order. Average again.

WORKSHOP RESOURCE >>

Average height/age chart for adult women or men
http://www.halls.md/chart/height-weight.htm

> Study adult siblings and compare their heights. The more people you survey, the more accurate your statistics will be.

CONSIDER THIS! PRESENT THIS!

> Graph your results. Average your results for oldest children, middle children, and youngest children, and create bars that represent these averages. You may wish to divide your subjects by gender.

> GO THE EXTRA MILE! Your pediatrician has a children's growth chart in the file of each patient. Next time you have a physical, ask to take a look at yours.

BIRTH ORDER AND WHAT WE DO

(Look for connections between actions, activities, and birth order)

TIME NEEDED >
two weeks

SCIENCE > sociology, statistics, health, education, economics

SCIENCE CONCEPTS >
statistical analysis, sociology

ADULT INVOLVEMENT >
Your high school athletic director can help you check rosters of athletes to find families with two or more siblings. You will need to ask permission to include fellow students in your study. Remember to comply with all legal guidelines, including ISEF rules. See the resources section for links.

the basics

SCIENTISTS SUCH as Daniel Rees access the National Survey of Youth, the National Educational Longitudinal Study, and other "microdata sets" compiled by the government. By looking at these large data sets, they see patterns emerge. The data sets are all based on questionnaires or interviews.

the buzz

Daniel Rees, Elizabeth Lopez, and a team at the University of Colorado at Denver showed that birth order was linked to positive effects—participation in school activities—as well as negative effects—nonparticipation, or becoming involved in risky activities such as smoking, drinking, and sex. Boys with older siblings were more likely to be involved in football, baseball, cheerleading, or swim teams and less likely to take part in music, art, or dance. Girls with older siblings participated less in band, yearbook, and community service. And kids with older brothers and sisters were found to be more likely to try risky things than oldest kids and only children.

the QUESTION >> Is the connection between birth order and activities evident in your school? Survey siblings in your local high school to learn who plays what sports and what positions they play.

the PLAN >> Find raw data on participation in activities, and look for connections between participation and family size and birth order.

> **"**
> *I've always been interested in behaviors.* **What makes people behave as they do?**
> **"**

— Daniel Rees,

He became an economist because it was a way of using numbers to find links between behaviors and other information about a person that could give clues to the why behind the what.

the lingo

statistical analysis—studying numbers to discover relationships and patterns

data sets—the results of an observation or study, usually in numbers

you'll need

help from your local high school's office to contact families with siblings

questionnaire

a computer spreadsheet program such as Excel

what to do

1 **USE A DATABASE** of lists of names, such as the rosters or membership lists of school clubs or teams.

2 **USE THE SCHOOL** directory to identify and get in touch with freshmen or sophomores with

siblings in the school. Although Rees's work dealt with figures on high school students, you can write your own survey—or search the Internet—for statistics on middle schoolers or any other age group.

3 **ASK STUDENTS TO** take part in your study. If they agree, send them your questionnaire. Your questionnaire should ask family size and birth order.

4 **USE THE SPREADSHEET** program to input your responses. Create three columns for every available student activity: oldest, middle, and youngest. Enter a 1 for each student polled who participates in each activity, in the correct column for birth order. (If you have a student who participates in four activities, you will enter a 1 for that student in the birth order column for each of the four activities.) When you are

Soccer Oldest (O)	Soccer Middle (M)	Soccer Youngest (Y)	Art O	Art M	Art Y	Judo O	Judo M	Judo Y

finished with this input, the program can help you total the number of oldest, middle, and youngest siblings who participate in each activity.

5 **ASSESS YOUR OUTCOMES.** What other factors might be involved in activity participation within each family? Such as, does having an older sibling play baseball make it more likely that a younger sibling will? What other information might you look for in determining whether participation is solely linked to birth order?

WORKSHOP RESOURCES >>

Bureau of Labor Statistics longitudinal survey page
http://www.bls.gov/nls/

National Center for Education Statistics, Education Longitudinal Study of 2002 page
http://nces.ed.gov/surveys/ELS2002/

> Daniel Rees passes on this statistician's trick: If you think people might lie about their answers, tell all your respondents to flip a coin before they answer your question. Heads, they have to tell the truth. Tails, they have to tell the opposite of the truth. Ask them not to tell the outcome of their coin flip. This method ensures that equal portions of people will tell the truth and lie, but the researcher won't be able to tell which is which. This allows subjects to feel that their privacy is safe.

CONSIDER THIS! PRESENT THIS!

> Place jars on your presentation table for sports, band, yearbook, theater, student government, community service, and other activities you can think of. Use dried beans of three different colors to represent oldest, middle, and youngest—for example green peas for oldest, red kidney beans for middle, white fava beans for youngest. Ask everyone who passes by your table to put an appropriately colored bean into each of the jars for activities he or she was involved with in middle school or high school. The levels of participation by people of different birth orders in different activities will be easy to see.

> **GO THE EXTRA MILE!** Interview the adviser of an activity you studied to tell him or her the results of your study. What is the adviser's interpretation of your results?

FACES OF TWINS

(Study people's ability to distinguish between identical twins)

TIME NEEDED >
one week

SCIENCE >
psychology, education

SCIENCE CONCEPT >
categorical induction

ADULT INVOLVEMENT >
written consent for use of pictures of subjects. Remember to comply with all legal guidelines including ISEF rules. See the resources section for links.

the basics

IN THIS EXPERIMENT, you'll study whether people can tell identical twins apart. Some identical twins are more alike than others, making them more difficult to tell apart. This may be because they shared a placenta, the organ that supplies blood as the baby develops in the uterus. Only 30 percent of identical twins have their own placentas.

the buzz

British psychologist Sarah Stevenage conducted studies in which she trained subjects to tell the difference between sets of identical twins. What happened when people were asked to distinguish between genetically identical faces depended on how they were taught to tell the twins apart and how long the teaching and testing went on. Stevenage concluded that people trying to distinguish between identical twins acquired two skills: learning to tell the twins apart and learning to name each twin. Acquiring both skills is described as mastering categorical induction.

the lingo

monozygotic (MG, or identical) twins are identical because they came from the same egg, which divided to form two distinct babies. They are always the same gender, but even "identical" twins are not always exactly alike. **dizygotic (DG, or fraternal) twins** were formed from separate eggs, making them no more alike genetically than brothers or sisters born separately.

> " *Monozygotic twins' parents and siblings have* **little difficulty in telling twins apart.** *Categorical perception experiments may explain why:* **Parents and siblings may master categorical induction before everyone else.** "

— Nancy L. Segal,
director of the Twin Studies Center at California State University

the QUESTION >> Can people distinguish between identical twins?

the PLAN >> Psychologist Nancy L. Segal suggested this study, in which she uses normal and reversed photographs to help subjects tell the difference between mirror images of one twin and images of two twins side by side.

you'll need

photos of a set of identical twins
(or several sets): Take your own,
getting permission from parents to
use the pictures, or use sets of twin
pictures found on the Internet. (If
you do this, be sure to credit the
source of the photos.)
a camera
a computer with a photo
organization program such as
Photoshop or iPhoto

what to do

1 **PHOTOGRAPH THE TWINS.**
For each set of twins, take
three photographs of each twin,
being careful to keep the background
and lighting the same: front view,
left profile, and right profile.

2 **ASSEMBLE FOUR PHOTO**
pairs, using a computer
photo organization program such
as Photoshop. Some images will be
the original photos you took; others
will be reversed or "flipped" photos,
which are mirror images of your
originals. Note that not all picture
pairs should show both twins! Some
should just be two images of the
same twin. For example,

A. original front views of Donna and
   Daisy
B. original front view of Donna and
   reversed front view of Donna
C. original front view of Donna and
   reversed front view of Daisy
D. reversed front view of Donna and
   reversed front view of Daisy

NOTE: *Keep a key for yourself that
tells you who's who!*

3 **ASK YOUR SUBJECTS** to study the pairs of pictures and tell which pairs are the same person and which are different people.

4 **HAVE YOUR SUBJECTS** give each pair a rating from 1 to 5, in which 1 is most similar and 5 is least similar.

5 **COMPARE THE SUBJECTS'** ratings. Which pair of photographs was judged to be the most alike?

6 **YOU CAN ASK** your twins to rate the similarities, too. Ask them to identify themselves in each picture. Do they think they are most similar to their original picture, their reverse image, or their twin's reverse image?

7 **IF YOU LIKE,** ask their families and friends to look at the pictures, too.

WORKSHOP RESOURCES >>

How Twins Work
http://science.howstuffworks.com/twin.htm

"Studying Nature vs. Nurture: Designing a Genetic Experiment," Discovery School
http://streaming.discoveryeducation.com/teacherCenter/
lessonPlans/pdfs/6-8_
StudyingNatureVsNurtureDesigningAGeneticExperiment.pdf

> Find out whether your twins are both right-handed or left-handed (hand concordant) or have different handedness (hand discordant). Twenty-five percent of identical twins are hand discordant—and may be easier to tell apart . . . or are they?

CONSIDER THIS! PRESENT THIS!

> Take pictures of celebrities, teachers, students, administrators and other people that everyone at your science fair will recognize. Reverse them, and display the reverse and the original side by side, either in printouts or as a slide show. Ask visitors to identify the original picture and the flipped photo, and tally the answers. Include your photographs of twins, and ask people to identify who's who.

> GO THE EXTRA MILE! Twins are not mirror images of each other. But they might think they are since, like most of us, they are more familiar with their own mirror images than their true images. Try flipping a photograph of yourself and placing it next to the original. Which one do you think looks most like you?

TWINS AND OTHER SIBLINGS

(Compare the abilities of different pairs of siblings to negotiate with each other)

TIME NEEDED >
one week

SCIENCE >
evolutionary psychology,
biology, game theory

SCIENCE CONCEPTS >
behavioral genetics:
personality and individual
differences, biological
relationships

ADULT INVOLVEMENT >
None needed. Remember
to comply with all legal
guidelines, including ISEF
rules. See the resources
section for links.

the basics

GAME THEORISTS try to understand what strategies people use to win in certain situations. Studies of sibling behavior have helped them understand evolutionary psychology, behaviors that help individuals survive.

the buzz

Twin studies frequently help scientists determine whether traits are dictated by biology or environment. Psychologist Nancy L. Segal, director of the Twin Studies Center at California State University, Fullerton, gives questionnaires to twin siblings and single-birth siblings. Which siblings see most eye-to-eye when they try to come up with answers that both can agree on? The results help game theorists, psychologists, and others understand what biology and behavior are involved when two people try to meet the same goal. Segal has included more than 120 pairs of virtual twins in her study.

the lingo

virtual twins—siblings who are no more than nine months apart in age

Of the virtual twins Nancy Segal has studied, 75 percent are two adoptees, and 25 percent are one adopted child and one biological child. Both combinations are virtual twins.

> *I have a **fraternal twin sister**. She looks nothing like me! Identical twins I knew at school were so close and had so much fun. I've always been fascinated that my sister and I were so different from each other, and **that set my path to study the twin phenomenon.***

— When Nancy L. Segal was a kid

the QUESTION >> How similar are siblings, and how good are they at predicting each other's answers?

the PLAN >> Question pairs of siblings as they try to anticipate each other's answers, and compare their responses.

Question	Condition A: What's your answer for yourself?	Condition B: What answer would you and your sibling agree on?
1. Write down any year, past or present or future.		
2. Name any flower.		
3. Name any car manufacturer.		
4. Write down any day of the year.		
5. Name any town or city.		
6. Write down any positive number.		
7. Write down any number.		
8. Write down any boy's name.		
9. Complete the sentence: A coin was tossed. It came down _____.		
10. Complete the sentence: The doctor asked for the patient's records. The nurse gave them to ____.		

you'll need

a group of siblings, whoever is around you. If possible, include identical twins, fraternal twins, and virtual twins, as well as other sibling pairs.
Questionnaire (see box)

what to do

1 PRE-INTERVIEW EACH PAIR of siblings, gathering the following data:

A. What's your birth date?
B. Describe your relationship to each other. Are you
   a. _____ single-born siblings,
   b. _____ adopted siblings,
   c. _____ virtual twins,
   d. _____ fraternal twins,
   e. _____ identical twins?
C. If you're twins, answer each question:
   a. Are you alike as two peas in a pod?
   b. Did your parents confuse you when you were babies?
   c. Do people meeting you for the first time confuse you?
   d. What is your hair color?
   e. What is your eye color?
   f. What is your height?
   g. What is your weight?

2 GIVE THE QUESTIONNAIRE to the pairs of siblings. Place siblings across the room from one another so they can't exchange looks

Nancy Segal credits these questions to J. Mehta, C. Starmer, and R. Sugden.*

* "Big Answers from Little People" by David Dobbs, *Scientific American,* September 2, 2005.

or communicate in any way. Have your subjects answer the questions twice. First, in the column for Condition A, ask them to answer the questions for themselves; then, in the column for Condition B, for them both. They should answer not as they think their sibling will answer, but as the two of them would answer if they could negotiate an answer. For example, if the question were favorite ice cream, one might answer chocolate, and the other vanilla. But the two together could agree on strawberry.

3 **FOR EACH PAIR,** tally their matching answers. Compare the number of correct answers for each different category of siblings.

WORKSHOP RESOURCE >>

http://psych.fullerton.edu/nsegal/twins

> Nancy L. Segal knows about the theory that twins use mental telepathy to communicate, but she asserts that no scientific studies demonstrate this ability. "Twins match highly in intelligence, special abilities, and problem-solving skills. But most identical twins don't pretend to read each other's minds. Why do they buy the same outfit? Look at the reason anybody buys an outfit: color, feel, style, cost. It's nothing to do with extrasensory perception. There are many better explanations we can make: the more genes siblings have in common, the more they relate to the world in the same way."

CONSIDER THIS! PRESENT THIS!

> Try the questionnaire on pairs of people with special bonds, such as a married couple or two best friends. Include them in a bar graph showing the matches between responses in your questionnaire.

> **GO THE EXTRA MILE!** Contribute your answers to Nancy L. Segal's study: nsegal@fullerton.edu

WHAT DO YOU SEE?

(Find out what your baby brother or sister can see)

TIME NEEDED >
two or three days

SCIENCE >
physiology, child development, optometry

SCIENCE CONCEPTS >
growth and development of vision, forced-choice study

ADULT INVOLVEMENT >
written permission to work with a baby, and assistance interacting with him or her. Remember to comply with all legal guidelines including ISEF rules. See the resources section for links.

the basics

IN THE PAST, people thought babies couldn't see or make sense of the pea soup of sensory information that the world presented to them, but information from baby researchers is changing theories about how and when processing of sensory information develops.

the buzz

Dr. Rowan Candy of the Infant Vision Laboratory at Indiana University led a group that studied how clearly babies see and what they look at. It concluded that vision development is linked to brain growth. Candy showed that babies of three months and older can focus on objects held at different distances from their eyes. By the time babies are six months old or more, they meet the eyes of parents and siblings as they come in the door. Candy's research has been conducted on even younger babies through an EEG test involving sensors, a special camera, and the simple picture method used in this workshop.

the lingo

forced-choice preference—a tool for giving subjects a limited number of things to look at

you'll need

a baby
two 4 x 6 white index cards
black permanent marker
notebook
white cardboard (poster board is fine) approximately 20˝ x 24˝ (long enough for the images to be

the QUESTION >> What can your newborn baby brother or sister see? Can he or she tell the difference between two patterns?

the PLAN >> Create or copy two patterns and present them to the baby, observing which he or she looks at first, second, shortest, and longest.

separate, high enough for the board to block out the background)

OPTIONAL: *video camera*

what to do

1 **MAKE PATTERN CARDS.**
Use the marker to draw black stripes on the white index card, as shown in the drawing. Color the other card completely black. Attach the cards to opposite ends of the poster board.

2 **SHOW BOTH CARDS** to the baby. Prop your poster board up against a background. Make sure the background is not so interesting that the baby might look there instead. A blank wall is good. Also notice the lighting. If you hold your

board up in front of a window, light from the window might backlight the board, making its edge more interesting than the pictures on it.

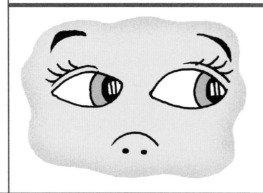

> You can also place an image that is all one color alongside the same image in which one part is colored differently. The baby's response can indicate color vision.

> Compare two black-and-white images: one stripes, the other a simple face. Try to draw the two images so that they have the same amount of black and white coloration; otherwise, the baby may prefer the one with the most coloration, and you won't learn what sort of image he or she prefers.

CONSIDER THIS! PRESENT THIS!

> Write up your observation, describing the baby's response. Along with your time measurements, your report should show the criteria you used in determining the baby's preference, such as length of eye contact, reaching, or laughing.

> **GO THE EXTRA MILE!** Try these pattern comparisons with older babies of different ages to see if their preferences differ.

3 **NOTE HOW LONG** the baby looks at each card. Watch the baby's eyes as they move between the cards, noting how long he or she focuses on each one, how many times he or she looks back and forth between them, and so on.

4 **NOTICE WAYS** the baby indicates a preference. Candy says babies look back and forth between images before paying more attention to one than the other. Older babies may smile, laugh, or lean toward or reach toward the preferred image.

5 **OPTIONAL: VIDEOTAPE THE** baby's response to the cards.

6 **REPEAT THIS EXERCISE** later and see if things change. Candy says that repeating ten times is an indication of pattern preference.

WORKSHOP RESOURCES >>

Infant Visual Development Lab home page and images that show what a baby sees at different ages
http://www.opt.indiana.edu/people/faculty/candy/index.html

You can even have your baby brother or sister take part in the research being done at the Infant Visual Development Lab by contacting Dr. Rowan Candy:
rcandy@indiana.edu

Tiny Eyes
http://tinyeyes.com/

WHAT A BABY LIKES
(Do babies prefer what they know?)

the basics

AS WITH THE VISUAL LAB in Workshop 5, babies' preferences can be demonstrated by which object they look at the most. By comparing the preferences of a number of babies as young as three months old, scientists begin to make generalizations about how preferences develop.

TIME NEEDED >
one day to one week (depending on how you schedule babies)

SCIENCE > cognitive development, sociology

SCIENCE CONCEPT > brain research

ADULT INVOLVEMENT > You'll need written permission to work with babies, and assistance interacting with them. Remember to comply with all legal guidelines, including ISEF rules. See the resources section for links.

the buzz

Elizabeth Spelke's baby brain research lab at Harvard University has uncovered surprising information about the choices babies make. Although babies don't get to actually choose who they're with, Spelke has shown that their preferences are likely based on their experience. For example, a Spelke study found that Israeli babies who saw all white people preferred white faces, while the babies of Ethiopian immigrants to Israel, who saw black and white people, had no preference.

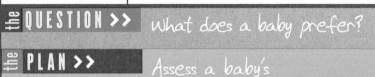

the QUESTION >> What does a baby prefer?

the PLAN >> Assess a baby's preference for gender by studying the faces he or she prefers.

the lingo

innate skills—skills you are born with
learned skills—skills you learn through experience

you'll need

your baby brother or sister and some of his or her friends
pictures of babies—Post them on your computer screen in boy/girl pairs, side by side.

OPTIONAL: Print the pictures out and place them on a poster side by side.

what to do

1 **SETUP:** Use a dimly lit room so the computer will catch the baby's eye. Set things up so the baby will be sitting only 18 to 24 inches from the computer, farther away if your babies are older than six months. You may need to experiment to find out what distance is best for a particular age group.

NOTE: *It may be easiest to have a mother or father hold the baby in his or her lap. The parents may be most comfortable with this.*

2 TESTING: For each baby you test, show at least five pairs of baby pictures. Note carefully which picture the baby looks at longest.

3 ANALYZE DATA: For each baby, use your data to figure out which of each pair of pictures was preferred: boy or girl. Come up with a percentage that gives your outcome. What percent of the five pictures the baby preferred were the same gender as he or she?

WORKSHOP RESOURCE >>

For more on Elizabeth Spelke's work, see the website for the Laboratory for Developmental Studies at Harvard University http://www.wjh.harvard.edu/~lds/

> ❝
> *I think like a*
> **three-year-old.**
> ❞

— Elizabeth Spelke, describing how she comes up with simple preference tests for babies

> What conclusions could you draw (such as babies do or do not prefer their same gender in pictures of babies) about the preferences you tested for?

CONSIDER THIS! PRESENT THIS!

Graph your results, using a bar graph to show preferences. Feeling corny? Add pink or blue to your graph to show your babies and their preferences.

GO THE EXTRA MILE! What other preferences could you test babies for?

YOU'VE GOT IT OR YOU DON'T
(Map the DNA for a special taste gene)

TIME NEEDED >
two or more days

SCIENCE >
biology, genetics

SCIENCE CONCEPTS >
heredity, DNA

ADULT INVOLVEMENT >
Get permission from the parent of any child to whom you give something to eat or taste, and have the parents present. Remember to comply with all legal guidelines, including ISEF rules. See the resources section for links.

the basics

WHAT MAKES you who you are? Your genes. Humans have about 30,000 genes. Chromosomes from each parent pair off to make your genes. The way these chromosomes combine creates your "genetic code"—the plans for the design of your body. DNA is the substance that makes up chromosomes.

the buzz

Compare any two people and you'll find that almost every bit of their DNA is the same. It's human DNA, not butterfly or bat DNA, after all. But it's that tiny percentage of DNA (under one tenth of one percent!) that accounts for all the differences between our looks, our personalities, and all that we are and do. Siblings (other than identical twins) share only 50 percent of each other's genes.

If you mate two rats, each with a dominant and a recessive gene, you may have black rats with two black fur alleles, black rats with one black fur allele and one (recessive) white allele, and white rats with two white fur alleles.

the lingo

allele: a gene for a specific trait, such as fur color or PTC tasting
phenylthiocarbamide (PTC): a chemical that tastes not-so-great to about 75 percent of humans; the remaining 25 percent don't taste anything at all. There's a gene linked to tasting PTC, so finding out whether you can taste the chemical is an indication of the gene's presence in your personal blueprint, your deoxyribonucleic acid, or DNA.

the QUESTION >> Which of your family members have the taste allele for PTC?

the PLAN >> You'll fill out a Punnett square like this for your family's PTC taste.

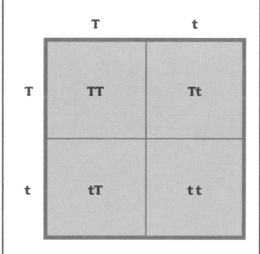

TT: both parents passed down a taste allele; both parents could taste PTC

Tt: one parent passed down a taste allele; only one parent could taste PTC

tt: neither parent passed down a taste allele; neither parent could taste PTC

you'll need

PTC taste strips—Note that you can cut one strip into pieces. See resources below for one source.
paper and pen or computer program that allows you to create graphics
family members—the more the better. If possible, try for at least three generations by involving your grandparents and great grandparents, as well as aunts, uncles, and cousins.

what to do

1 **DO THE TASTE TEST.** Ask each family member to place the PTC strip in his or her mouth and wait a few seconds. They will either taste something strong (and, some say, a little unpleasant) or nothing at all. Record the responses.

2 **WHEN YOU HAVE TESTED** as many family members as possible, map who said yes and who said no. Refer to the Punnett square on page 31 for help in figuring out the combination of taste alleles each family member has in his or her DNA.

> How does your family's percentage of the PTC taste alleles compare to the percentage in the general population? (Seventy-five percent have at least one taste allele.)

CONSIDER THIS! PRESENT THIS!

> Invite families attending your science fair to test their PTC-tasting ability at your table. Make Punnett squares for them.

> GO THE EXTRA MILE! You may also test other families to compare them with your own.

WORKSHOP RESOURCES >>

You can learn more about this experiment and see what your DNA for PTC tasting looks like at the Stanford University website
http://med.stanford.edu/news_releases/2003/february/bitter.html

Genetic taste test strips
http://www.fishersci.com/
Search for "taste test."

IT'S GENETIC... OR IS IT?

(Determine if we get our food preferences from our families)

the basics

GENETIC TRAITS are mapped through a family tree. They help to clearly layout different characteristics such as the likes and dislikes illustrated here:

TIME NEEDED > one day to one week, depending on the number of people you include in your study

SCIENCE > biology, genetics, biopsychology

SCIENCE CONCEPTS > heredity, the nature/nurture question

ADULT INVOLVEMENT > Needed. Remember to comply with all legal guidelines, including ISEF rules. See the resources section for links.

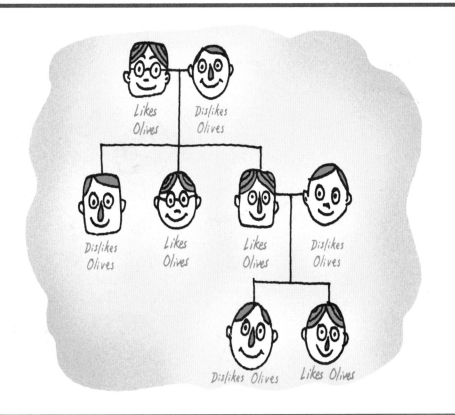

the buzz

Biopsychologist Julie Mennella of the Monell Chemical Senses Center in Philadelphia combined psychology and biology when she studied the responses of 143 mother-and-child pairs to bitter substances. Her lab extracted each person's DNA and came up with three genotypes (characteristics caused by genes), based on whether or not a child had what she called the "bitter gene"—either from both parents or just one. If the bitter gene was called P, a child could be PP (both parents), Pp (one parent), or pp (neither parent). PP children were most sensitive—and turned off by—bitter tastes, and they preferred sweet things.

the lingo

genetic traits—traits that are passed down through the genes from parents
learned traits—traits that are often caused by family or cultural influences, but they can have some biological influences, too.

you'll need

information about your family members
pencil and paper or a computer program that allows you to make a map like the one on page 33
method for communicating with family members: e-mail, phone, face-to-face interview
notebook

the QUESTION >> Can liking something—such as olives—be traced through families? Is it an inherited (genetic) trait?

the PLAN >> Write a questionnaire about a food preference to see whether the taste for a food runs within families. For instance, do you like olives? Use your data to map the trait through your family tree, and try to infer whether the trait is passed down through nature (genetically) or learned (family practice).

what to do

1 PICK A TRAIT. Question or study your own family to learn who has that particular trait. There are many traits you can study, and this approach can be applied to, for example:

FOOD *preferences—pickles, olives, dark or milk chocolate, maple syrup on pancakes, sauce on spaghetti, etc.*

APPEARANCE—*eye color, ear lobes (attached directly to the head or hanging down), cleft in chin, curly hair, dimples, second toe longer than the first*

PHYSICAL ABILITY—*tongue rolling, left- or right-handedness, crossing left thumb over right when you fold your hands*

ARTISTIC TALENT—*musical ability, drawing ability*

PHYSICAL TRAITS—*allergies, color blindness*

2 MAP THE TRAIT through your own family to see how dominant (or not) it is. Which parent do you think each child got the trait from?

"

In understanding **food preferences,** *I studied babies. Babies experience tastes from foods their mothers eat when pregnant or breastfeeding.* **And the more a child is exposed to a certain food, the more she'll eat it.**

"

— Julie Mennella,
Monell Chemical Senses Center

> Compare the percentage of people in your family with a certain trait to the percentage of people in the general public with the trait. Use this formula: (number with trait) ÷ (number in group) x 100 = ___ percent of group with the trait

> To find general public percentages, visit the National Institute of Health's website, Online Mendelian Inheritance in Man, at http://www.ncbi.nlm.nih.gov/omim/

CONSIDER THIS! PRESENT THIS!

> Present your results as a bar graph or family tree. For a bar graph, simply create a color symbol for the trait, and add one symbol to the bar for each person who has that trait. For example, if you use an olive to show who likes olives, and ten people like olives, your bar graph will show ten olives in the "likes olives" bar. The most prevalent traits will be represented by the longest column (bar) of symbols.

> GO THE EXTRA MILE! Extend the questionnaire to other families, and see how the answers map out.

3 **EXPAND YOUR DATABASE.** Write a question or two about experiences that might contribute to this trait (especially food preference)—for example, getting food poisoning, having a favorite relative make a special dish for you, or having an allergic reaction. Determine if the answer will add to the information about whether this is a genetic or learned trait.

4 **WHAT CONCLUSIONS** can you draw about the dominance of the gene that dictates these preferences? Does it seem dominant or recessive? Is it a learned or genetic trait, or both?

WORKSHOP RESOURCE >>

What Is a Gene?
http://www.thetech.org/genetics/feature.php

EATING IN THE FAMILY GROUP

(Does who you eat with affect how much you eat?)

the basics

BOUT THE TIME of the Ice Age, humans began to kill and eat large animals. Groups of people living together—most often families—learned to work together to find food. They developed a group mentality that helped them coordinate their efforts against dangerous animals. But they also developed another mentality—one that dictated that they compete for the food that was available.

TIME NEEDED >
two or more days

SCIENCE > behavioral
psychology

SCIENCE CONCEPT >
effect of group size on
eating habits

ADULT INVOLVEMENT >
You will need permission
from parents or school
administration. (But you
don't need to do your
research in a school
setting.) Remember to
comply with all legal
guidelines, including ISEF
rules. See the resources
section for links.

the buzz

Julie C. Lumeng and Katherine H. Hillman of the University of Michigan fed preschoolers in small and large groups and found that the more individuals there are in a group, the more each group member ate. The scientists offered graham crackers to children in groups of three to nine, and did the same with groups of thirty. The children in the larger groups ate 30 percent more than the ones in the small group.

you'll need

Lunches for your test group for several days. Read through "what to do" to assess how much and what food you'll need.

what to do

1 **INVITE SIX TO TEN** classmates to be part of your research project. Divide them

> **In animals, you're going to be a little more frenzied when you eat in a group.**

— Julie C. Lumeng,
University of Michigan

into two groups. Tell them that this project involves having lunch with you for two days in one week. You might do this during a school vacation at home or in school (with school permission). Check with your subjects about food allergies, and, in the interest of science, rule out any subject with restrictions.

2 **PLAN YOUR EATING SETTINGS:**
A. Serve lunch on the first day to a group of three or four people. You may need to arrange a setting for this: an empty classroom, a nook in the cafeteria, or picnic table outside.

the QUESTION >> Can you replicate Lumeng and Hillman's experiment with your family or school group? Will people eat more in a group than they eat alone?

the PLAN >> Replicate their experiment or try the middle school adaptation below.

It's important that this small group setting be separate from other people.

B. On the second day, serve lunch to the second group of three or four people.

C. On the next day, serve lunch to the two groups together.

3 PLAN THE FOOD:

A. Buy and/or bring in lunch for all of your subjects. Place the food in the center of the table or on a separate table and invite everyone to help themselves. Try to provide more food than you think people will eat.

NOTE: *Be sure to follow school rules about bringing food for other kids.*

B. Be sure to provide the same amount of food for each of the first two lunches you serve.

4 SERVE THE LUNCHES. You may record what gets eaten, or just count what's left at the end of the lunch.

5 COMPARE THE AMOUNT of food eaten at each lunch.

WORKSHOP RESOURCES >>

Family Doctor page on keeping a food diary
http://familydoctor.org/online/famdocen/home/healthy/food/general-nutrition/299.html

Blank food diaries to print out are available at
http://weightloss.about.com/od/emotionsmotivation/a/fooddiary.htm

> Do you think the number of people you're with will affect the amount you eat?

CONSIDER THIS! PRESENT THIS!

> Gather and present information for the groups, or use pseudonyms (call a subject Person A, or give him or her a phony name) to describe the different behavior of individuals in groups of different sizes.

> GO THE EXTRA MILE! Lumeng suggests keeping a week's food diary (in which you write down everything you eat) that includes a notation of the number of people who were around when you ate. You might even keep track of the specific people present. Is there anyone who inspires you to eat more than others?

WATCH THIS!

(Videotape and analyze sibling discussions)

TIME NEEDED ›
several weeks to a month

SCIENCE › psychology

SCIENCE CONCEPTS ›
behavior, observation,
analysis of observation,
scales

ADULT INVOLVEMENT ›
Get permission to
videotape two siblings
discussing a conflict
or issue between them.
Follow your science fair
committee's require-
ments and comply with
all legal guidelines,
including ISEF rules. See
the resources section
for links. You must be
committed to keeping
conversations private.

the basics

BROTHERS AND SISTERS often find themselves in conflict over certain areas or issues. Sibling conflict may be stronger when siblings are close in age. Identifying different methods of dealing with conflict may shed light on how some siblings resolve problems.

the buzz

A study by Annie McNerney and Joy Usner asked 85 college students to rate the intensity and kind of rivalry (academic, social, and physical) they experienced with their siblings at different ages. They found that sibling rivalry is most pronounced between the ages of 10 and 15. And, in a study of 300 Pittsburgh boys from birth to age 17, Daniel Shaw and his team found that unusually difficult sibling relationships were frequently linked to deviant behavior and other trouble with the law.

the lingo

sibling rivalry—Many scientists agree that sibling conflict stems from competition.

you'll need

a video camera and computer or TV for viewing the video
several pairs of siblings
copies of the Sibling Relationship Questionnaire (page 43)
a team of observers (three is a good number) with different birth orders in their families. (For instance, you don't want to include all youngest siblings. Find people with different family positions.) These people may be adults or other kids, but don't include your own siblings.

the QUESTION >> What happens when siblings discuss a touchy subject?

the PLAN >> Interview siblings separately to find issues for them to discuss while being videotaped. Then assess the video and rate the interaction using a scale created by psychologists.

You can do the prevideo and video sessions yourself, then bring in your observers for the postvideo session. **copies of the Sibling Global Scale** (a system for rating observations—see page 43)

what to do

PREVIDEO: *Before you begin,*

1 **CREATE ENOUGH SIBLING** Relationship Questionnaires for each sibling to have one.

2 **SET UP** a video area in a private place with two chairs and a table in between.

3 **OBTAIN FULL UNDERSTANDING** and permission from each pair of siblings and their parents about the way your study will be conducted.

4 **GIVE THEM** the Sibling Relationship Questionnaire.

5 **STUDY THE QUESTIONNAIRE** results to find an area that you think is a source of conflict for both siblings. If there is no one area in common, choose one topic from each sibling's answers and have them discuss it. Jot the topic selected for discussion on a card. (Use two cards if you choose two topics.)

VIDEO: *For each pair you study, go through the following steps:*

6 **TAKE THE SIBLINGS** to the area you have set up for videotaping. For each topic, tell them you're going to ask them to discuss what's on the card for eight minutes. Ask them to read the card together, and then begin talking. Tell them that at the end of the time you'll

stop them. If they finish discussing the topic before you stop them, they should just keep on talking—either about the topic, or about something else—until the time is up.

7 **REPEAT** with the other topic, if necessary.

8 **CREATE ENOUGH COPIES** of the Sibling Global Scale for your observers to have one for each video interaction.

9 **ASSEMBLE YOUR TEAM** of observers, at least three people who agree to keep the videos confidential. Have them watch each video once or twice and assign ratings to the sibling pair, using the Sibling Global Scale.

10 **COMPILE THE RESULTS** for each video, discussing as needed with your team. Compare and contrast the discussion styles of the pair: Calm? Aggressive? Uninterested? What conclusions can you draw about the individuals and their relationship?

> Daniel Shaw looks for links between childhood relationships with siblings and later, adult behaviors or activities. What kind of results do you think he might find?

CONSIDER THIS! PRESENT THIS!

> Create graphs for each set of siblings that compare the results of the questionnaires and the observations.

> GO THE EXTRA MILE! Include yourself and a sibling in your study, having members of your observation team question, videotape, and rate your interaction. Where do you stand? Were you surprised by what they and you found?

WORKSHOP RESOURCES >>

Pitt Parents and Children Laboratory
www.pitt.edu/~ppcl

Sibling Rivalry in Degree and Dimensions Across the Lifespan, by Annie McNerney and Joy Usner,
http://jrscience.wcp.muohio.edu/humannature01/

SIBLING RELATIONSHIP QUESTIONNAIRE

(adapted from Sibling Relationship Questionnaire by Wendell Furman, University of Denver)

For each question: rate 1—5

1 *hardly at all*
2 *not too much*
3 *somewhat*
4 *very much*
5 *a great deal*

_____ How much do you and your sibling do nice things for each other?

_____ How much do you and your sibling go places and do things together?

_____ How much do you and your sibling try to outdo each other at things?

_____ How much do you and your sibling play around and have fun with each other?

_____ How much do you and your sibling disagree and quarrel with each other?

_____ How much do you and your sibling bug and pick on each other in mean ways?

For each question: rate 1—7

1 *more than once a day*
2 *every day*
3 *5—6 times in the last week*
4 *3—4 times in the last week*
5 *1—2 times in the last week*
6 *at least once this month*
7 *not at all in the last month*

_____ Your brother/sister got to do something and you didn't or was given something and you weren't.

_____ Your brother/sister took something of yours and wouldn't give it back.

_____ Your brother/sister messed up something in your room.

_____ You got in trouble for something your brother/sister did.

_____ Your brother/sister wouldn't let you play or do things with him/her and his/her friends, OR got in the way when you wanted to be with your friends.

_____ Your brother/sister told a lie and got you in trouble with your parents and/or friends.

SIBLING GLOBAL SCALE

(adapted from Sibling Global Scale provided by Daniel Shaw, University of Pittsburgh)

For each question: rate 1—5

1 *not at all*
2 *minimally*
3 *somewhat*
4 *moderately*
5 *mainly*

_____ How negative was the verbal or physical conflict?

_____ How positive was the relationship?

_____ How close do the siblings seem?

_____ How nice was sibling A?

_____ How nice was sibling B?

_____ How well did they address the problem?

_____ How bad was the issue talked about in the task?

FAVORITISM

(Study family favoritism among children)

TIME NEEDED > one day, but it's a long day, involving planning and carrying out observations in a public place

SCIENCE > sociology, behavioral psychology

SCIENCE CONCEPTS > observing and assessing patterns

ADULT INVOLVEMENT > For your observations, you'll need supervision, transportation, and assistance. You may need someone to time your observations while you take notes. Remember to comply with all legal guidelines, including ISEF rules. See the resources section for links.

the basics

IN PSYCHOLOGY, experiments are sometimes done on subjects, but research more often takes other forms, such as surveys, questionnaires, interviews, or observations.

the buzz

Laurie Kramer, a social scientist at the University of Illinois at Urbana-Champaign, worked with Amanda Cole to do studies with middle school siblings in which she assessed their treatment by parents.

the lingo

differential parental treatment—unequal treatment between siblings

you'll need

a good poker face (the ability to hide your reactions)
a notebook
a watch or two with second hands

OPTIONAL: *A partner can help you time parent engagement with children while you observe kinds of interactions. You can simply tell this person when to start and stop timing.*

what to do

1 **LAURIE KRAMER SAYS,** "Create a narrow scope." Look for three behaviors:
A. Observe activities. How does the parent talk to the child, direct the child, or do things for or help the child?
B. As much as possible, assess the content of the conversation.

the QUESTION >> Which child gets more attention from parents? What kind of attention does each child get?

the PLAN >> Observe a family (or several families) in a public place, assessing the amounts of time and kinds of attention spent on each child.

> "
> *Psychologists remember being the older or younger sibling, and* **we naturally have more sympathy for one or the other.** *So we have coders to watch tapes, to make sure we get an* **objective (fair) outcome.**
> "

— Daniel Shaw,
psychologist, University of Pittsburgh

Activities	Child 1	Child 2
Talking	× × ×	
Scolding		× ×
Consoling	×	
Directing		× ×
		×

"We've learned that lots of times when parents treat kids differently, the kids don't necessarily believe it's wrong. They say the parents have a reason, and if they have a reason, then it's not associated with a wrong outcome. The reason might be because they're different ages: An older sibling should have more privileges, the younger one should have more restrictions. There is also a perception of need; if they feel their sibling gets more attention they may feel that they need it. If it makes sense to them, they see it as fair." — Laurie Kramer

For more on Laurie Kramer's work with sibling relationships, see Workshop 12.

CONSIDER THIS! PRESENT THIS!

Consider illustrating your observations by making comic strips of interactions between parents and children. In the interest of privacy, use stick figures to show people, and use speech balloons to show what they are saying.

GO THE EXTRA MILE! Expand this study by narrowing your observations to families with certain things in common: for example, age spreads of the children, same-sex siblings, moms vs. dads, and so on. You'll need to expand the chart.

How much are parents giving instruction, scolding, consoling, just talking about something?

C. Note how much time the parent engages with each child. It may help to have a partner do this part, using two watches.

2 **DEVISE A CHART** with columns for two children, and rows for the different types of interactions you want to watch. See the chart above.

3 **IN YOUR NOTEBOOK,** write an entry that includes your general feeling about what you've observed about this family. Also note the time and location where your observation was made.

WORKSHOP RESOURCE >>

Laurie Kramer's web page
http://www.hcd.uiuc.edu/about/faculty_staff/l_kramer.html

CAN'T WE GET ALONG?

(Train siblings to resolve conflict)

the basics

CRITICAL SKILLS for developing positive sibling relationships include inviting play, refusing play, seeing things from the other person's perspective, solving problems, and dealing with emotions.

TIME NEEDED > at least two weeks

SCIENCE > behavioral psychology, educational psychology

SCIENCE CONCEPT > teaching young children to develop social and emotional competencies

ADULT INVOLVEMENT > You'll need permission from the parents of the children you're surveying. Get your science fair committee's rules and advice on this project before considering it and remember to comply with all legal guidelines, including ISEF rules. See the resources section for links.

the buzz

Laurie Kramer is a social scientist at the University of Illinois at Urbana-Champaign. In her lab, teachers work with young children in a preschool setting while parents watch (on TV) from another room. She has identified seven critical skills that are important for helping children develop positive relationships with their siblings. She developed ways to teach kids these skills; then she follows up to see the lasting effect of her teaching strategies.

the QUESTION >> Can you teach two siblings ways to resolve their conflicts?

the PLAN >> Over two or more weeks, show your preschool babysitting charges ways to resolve problems, and assess your success.

the lingo

role-play: a problem-solving technique in which participants play the roles of people in a conflict to explore different ways to resolve it

you'll need

regular access to two preschool siblings over a period of two weeks or more

cooperative parents who are willing not just to allow you to teach conflict resolution to their children but to back you up on it, reminding the children of your method.

what to do

1 **SHOW PRESCHOOLERS WHAT** you would like them to do when there is a problem between them. Here is the strategy to teach them:

A. Stop what you're doing when you recognize that there's a problem.

B. See it your way, see it my way. Explain your position and let the other person explain his or her position. Understand that you each have a different perception.

C. Think about what you want to have happen. Tell the other person.

D. Brainstorm to come up with one to three possible solutions.

E. Decide what to try to do. If you can't agree on an action to take together, drop it. Both of you move on to do something else instead— on your own or together.

2 **ROLE-PLAY, PRETENDING** there is a problem and walking the kids through the steps of the strategy. You *will* have to remind them of the strategy when they actually have a problem during play. Model a few solutions if kids have trouble coming up with some.

(One solution might be to take turns, for example).

3 **KEEP NOTES OF** what you do, what the kids do, how they respond to your guidance, and how many conflicts they go through with you before they repeat, know, or can implement the strategy themselves.

WORKSHOP RESOURCE >>

eHow page "How to Care for Three or More Children"
http://www.ehow.com/how_2118231_care-three-more-children.html?ref=fuel&utm_source=yahoo&utm_medium=ssp&utm_campaign=yssp_art

Laurie Kramer says that middle schoolers are often put in the position of taking care of little kids, but that they don't usually have strategies to help them. "They are given ambiguous (vague) instructions, such as 'take care of them, make sure they don't get in trouble'."

CONSIDER THIS! PRESENT THIS!

Write a brochure with the strategy that works for you in order to help other babysitters develop their skills with kids.

GO THE **EXTRA** MILE! Keep a journal of your own thoughts, feelings, and impressions as you work with the kids. What do your responses show you about yourself? How do you feel about your interaction with them? How could you change your approach to improve it? What might you do differently next time?

A HAND TO HOLD

(See if holding a loved one's hand eases stress)

TIME NEEDED >
a weekend

SCIENCE > neurology

SCIENCE CONCEPTS >
brain activity,
psychology, technology

ADULT INVOLVEMENT >
Get permission for
parents to use the
Stroop test with their
children. You may also
need help taking people's
pulses or learning how to
take a pulse. Follow your
science fair committee's
rules on using human
subjects. Remember
to comply with all legal
guidelines, including ISEF
rules. See the resources
section for links.

the basics

WHEN A PERSON is stressed by something perceived with the senses (through sight, sound, touch, taste, or smell), the alarm center of the brain causes stress hormones to be produced, which makes the person's heart beat faster.

the buzz

In 2006, neuroscientists found that women who hold their husbands' hands when they are under stress are calmed. This experiment was the first neural study of the effect of human touch on stress, meaning that the scientists used brain scans to watch changes in activity in the alarm centers of the brain in women who held their husbands' hands.

A Belgian study of kids with eating disorders found that having a brother or sister close by may speed up recovery. Siblings help therapists understand how the family works, act as role models for the sick kid, and give him or her a hand to hold.

the lingo

controlling variables—eliminating factors that could affect your outcome. This control allows you to eliminate these factors from your consideration as you try to figure out what's causing the pulse rate to rise or fall.

you'll need

color printer
Stroop test as found at the University of Washington's Neuroscience for Kids website: http://faculty.washington.edu/chudler/words.html

Print out a copy of the Stroop test and paste it onto cardboard, or use the test as a model to make individual cards (one per word), since it heightens stress to show just one word at a time. The subject has to name the colors, not read the words.

Level 1: words in the right colors
ORANGE   **BLUE**
Level 2: words in the wrong colors
ORANGE   **BLUE**

the QUESTION >> Does holding a sibling's hand make it easier to deal with stress?

the PLAN >> Give a stress test to siblings to learn whether or not having a brother or sister's hand to hold causes the pulse rate to rise or fall.

a watch or clock with a second hand for taking the pulse
ten sets of siblings—Control your variables by always having the older go first, finding pairs of siblings who are all the same gender, and finding pairs who are the same age difference.

what to do

1 **PRACTICE TAKING** a pulse. Learn to take your own

> "
The effect of this **simple gesture** [hand-holding] of social support is that the brain and body don't have to work as hard; **they're less stressed in response to a threat.**
"

— Dr. James A. Coan,

psychologist, University of Virginia

pulse, measured as the number of heartbeats per minute. Turn your hand palm up, and place the first two fingers of the other hand at your wrist just under the thumb. Find your pulse by pressing lightly. Once you can do this reliably, time your pulse: Count the heartbeats for 15 seconds, then multiply by 4 to get the heart rate per minute.

2 **FOR EACH OF** your subjects, you will take the pulse before and after exposing the subject to the Stroop test.

3 **DO ONE TEST,** selecting a sibling to focus on in all pairs: older or younger.

Take the subject's pulse before and after the test. The lower the pulse rate, the lower the stress level. Note, however, that people's regular pulses may vary. The key here is whether the difference in pulse before and after was less than, more than, or the same as those in the people whose hands were held.

4 **ASSESS YOUR FINDINGS.** What conclusions can you reach?

> Why do you think the Stroop test creates stress?

CONSIDER THIS! PRESENT THIS!

> Graph your results using a bar graph.

> **GO THE EXTRA MILE!** Find more pairs of subjects to test. You might compare the effect of making the tested subject the older or younger of the siblings. You might also see the effect of just having a sibling in the room, without holding hands. You can test your parents, too, or parent–child pairs.

WORKSHOP RESOURCE >>

How to Create a Stroop Effect Experiment
http://psychology.about.com/library/bl-stroopeffect.htm

LITTER WATCH

(Observe how puppies interact and how they establish group dominance)

the basics

THE **UNDERSTANDING** of social dynamics in animals centers on territory and establishing pecking order in the pack. The term "pecking order" comes from flocks of chickens, in which the boss chicken in a flock pecks all the chickens to which it considers itself superior, and each subordinate chicken does the same.

TIME NEEDED > one day

SCIENCE > sociology

SCIENCE CONCEPT > sociology of the group

ADULT INVOLVEMENT > Get permission to work with a litter of puppies. Follow your science fair committee's rules and advice about working with animals. Remember to comply with all legal guidelines, including ISEF rules. See the resources section for links.

the buzz

Understanding of social dynamics (interactions) and dominance (who's boss) in people has been studied extensively. Sociologists and other scientists work to understand gangs, warfare, human rights, and other large and small issues associated with groups.

the QUESTION >> Can you learn about pecking order through observing puppies?

the PLAN >> Observe a litter of puppies and analyze their order of social dominance. Note that pecking order isn't a static (established) situation. It may change as puppies grow older and continue jockeying for position in the litter.

the lingo

group—In sociology, a group is defined as a number of people with a shared characteristic. Primary groups are close, family-type groupings, usually involving blood relationships. A litter is an example of a primary group. So are you and your family. Secondary groups are people who are brought together because of shared location or goals, such as a town, the staff of a business, a class at school, or a scout troop.

you'll need

access to a litter of puppies
notebook and pen
OPTIONAL: *video camera, still camera*

what to do

1 **WATCH THE LITTER** from a distance. Keep a careful record of the interactions you observe. Photograph or videotape the puppies. Try to characterize or name the behaviors, including body language. You can also consult a book about dogs or an online dog source to see what animal behaviorists call these behaviors.

THINGS TO LOOK FOR
Ganging up: All the puppies go together to jump on an adult dog or another puppy; this litter is practicing working as a pack to attack prey. How do they coordinate their efforts?
Chewing on each other's heads: Notice which puppies bite each others' chins and which mouth the top of each other's heads or necks. The puppies fight to get the upper hand (or upper mouth) to establish dominance.
Dominant and submissive behaviors: Which puppy do you think is the big cheese? Which puppy is the tagalong? Which puppy is trying to push the big cheese off the throne? How can you tell? What do they do?

2 **THROW A TOY** into the middle of the litter and watch what they do. Which dog approaches the toy first? Next? Last?

3 **SIT DOWN IN** the middle of the litter. What happens? (Get someone to videotape this so that you can view it later and observe the puppies. Or have another person sit in the middle of the litter while you observe.)

4 **NOW SEPARATE TWO** puppies from the litter and give them a toy. What do they do? Which one dominates? Which one submits? Try with another two puppies. Use a bracket like the one shown here to keep track of the interactions between the puppies, having the dominant puppy be the winner. Continue pairing the puppies until you figure out their order of dominance.

WORKSHOP RESOURCES >>

Dog Owner's Guide on Pack Dynamics
http://www.canismajor.com/dog/packdyn.html

Digital Dog page "Pack Is Where the Heart Is"
http://www.digitaldog.com/pack.html

Humane Society of the United States website, Puppy Behavior Basics
http://www.hsus.org/animals/dogs/tips/puppy_behavior_basics.html

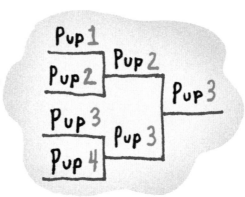

> Some animal behaviorists and dog trainers say that wolf pack dynamics shed light on how dogs behave in litters, packs, and family packs (which include humans) because wolves are closely related to dogs.

CONSIDER THIS! PRESENT THIS!

> Make a display copy of the bracket you use to keep track of your puppies. This can resemble the brackets used to keep track of and predict the outcome of a sports tournament such as the NCAA basketball tournament or the U.S. Open tennis tournament.

> Build your own bracket by typing in the number of teams at http://www.crowsdarts.com/brackets/playoff-chart.html. In this case, each puppy acts as its own team.

> GO THE **EXTRA** MILE! Have you heard the term "alpha dog"? Alpha is the first letter of the Greek alphabet. Find a copy of the Greek alphabet. Figure out the pecking order of your puppies and assign them each an appropriate Greek letter.

FAMILY FETCH

(Teach your dog to connect your siblings to their names and smells)

TIME NEEDED > four to seven days

SCIENCE > biology, physiology, animal behavior

SCIENCE CONCEPTS > senses, identification through odor

ADULT INVOLVEMENT > You'll need permission from a parent to teach the dog to identify family members through smell. Remember to comply with all legal guidelines, including ISEF rules. See the resources section for links.

the basics

DOGS ARE natural sniffers. The nose of a bloodhound (among the best of dog noses) has 220 million olfactory (smell) receptors, compared to a human's, which has about 20 million. Dogs' noses are 50 times more sensitive to smell than people's noses are.

the buzz

For safety's sake, dog trainer Brian Kilcommons recommends teaching your dog to find family members. Dogs professionally trained to sniff out humans, explosives, and drugs help make the world safer for people every day. There are thousands of "sniffer dogs" working in the United States today.

the lingo

positive reinforcement—This method of behavior modification involves rewarding desired behavior.

you'll need

a dog belonging to a family
at least two siblings or other members of that family
dog treats (hot dogs cut into slices work well)
T-shirts worn by the family members

what to do

1 **FIRST, TRY TO TEACH** your dog to find one sibling by saying her name. Here is the basic training that you will repeat until the dog can find your sibling wherever he or she is, within a limited area (such as your house or yard or a park). As you work, take note of how many times each step must be

the QUESTION >> Will your dog learn to find family members more quickly by name or by smell?

the PLAN >> Compare teaching your dog to find family members using their names with finding them using smell.

repeated before the dog grasps the concept and finds your sibling.
A. Say, "Find Anna." Do this with your sibling close by, holding a dog treat. At first, your sibling can hold out the treat to the dog.
B. Eventually, the sibling should sit with the dog treat hidden.
C. Later, she should be in another room.
D. Even later, she should be in another room or outside, *without* a dog treat. Try having your sibling hide under or behind something.
If your dog can find her on command, wherever she is, you can conclude that you've succeeded in teaching your dog to find this sibling. But can you teach him to find a different sibling?

Scientists in a team led by Yushan Yan, a chemical and environmental engineer at University of California, Riverside, are working on developing an electronic nose to detect explosives. Massachusetts Institute of Technology scientists are perfecting a smelling device that can detect gases, such as carbon monoxide.

CONSIDER THIS! PRESENT THIS!

Stage a demonstration at your science fair (first, get permission to bring your dog). Otherwise, show a video.

GO THE EXTRA MILE! Video your dog finding your siblings in a variety of situations, and add this data to your report.

2 **REPEAT THE TRAINING** with another sibling, using that sibling's name. How long did it take? Was the training needed more, less, or just as extensive as it was with the first person? Eventually, if your dog can find the correct person, you can conclude that you've succeeded in teaching him to differentiate between their names.

3 **YOU MIGHT TRAIN** the dog to find the person by name *and* smell, using a smelly T-shirt to help the dog identify the right person. Let the dog smell the shirt, and tell him the name of the person you want him to find. "Find Katie!" Eventually the dog will link the name with the smell and won't need to smell the T-shirt to follow your command. What difference do you think creating this extra link will make in the number of training repetitions needed?

WORKSHOP RESOURCES >>

If You Only Knew How Much I Smell You: True Portraits of Dogs *by Roy Blount, Jr.*

"How Police Dogs Work," How Stuff Works website
http://people.howstuffworks.com/police-dog4.htm

International Police K9 Conference website

http://www.policek9.com/

SMELLY SIBS

(Test your ability to identify your siblings' clothing by smell)

the basics

WE SHARE the most DNA with people who are related to us. Our senses tell us whether people are part of our kin or outsiders. How? Consider the way a body responds to a virus like the common cold: by identifying, isolating, and rejecting the invader. Our bodies can also identify noninvading cells—those possessed by people who are kin to us.

TIME NEEDED >
one or two days

SCIENCE >
biology, physiology

SCIENCE CONCEPTS >
human behavior, sensory perception, neuroscience (science of the brain)

ADULT INVOLVEMENT >
Permission may be needed for working with human subjects. Remember to comply with all legal guidelines, including ISEF rules. See the resources section for links.

the buzz

Researchers have shown that if you give a small child clothing worn by a newborn brother or sister, they recognize their sibling—even if they haven't yet met him or her. What good does this do a person? Scientists figure that families survive and thrive when they protect each other and work together, and that the instinct to do so begins by recognizing one's own kin.

the QUESTION >>

Can people identify family members by smell?

the PLAN >>

Match people with the clothes they've worn, using smell.

the lingo

olfactory nerve—This nerve carries information about odors received by olfactory receptors in the skin of the nose to the central nervous system.

you'll need

ten or more matching T-shirts, enough for each smelly participant
ten or more mailing envelopes, all the same size (enough for the shirts)
permanent marker
computer and printer for making answer sheets (or you can handwrite an answer sheet and make copies); you'll need an answer sheet for each smeller
smelly participants—people willing to wear one T-shirt all day through all of their activities
smellers—three or four people willing to try to identify all the smelly participants by sniffing their T-shirts (Smellers need to know all of the smelly participants.)

NOTE: *It's a good idea to do this experiment on a weekend. The key is to have the T-shirts worn all day the first day and to have all the smellers take the test the second day.*

what to do

1 **FIRST, FIGURE OUT** who your subjects will be. Explain the purpose of your experiment and the way the two days will work. Some subjects may be involved both days (if they are smelly participants and smellers), whereas others will be needed only for one day.

IMPORTANT: *Try to include family members and friends, siblings, parents, and other family members. Who do you think will turn out to be the best at identifying people by smell?*

2 **MAKE AN ANSWER** sheet for your smellers to use as

they try to identify the wearer of each T-shirt. The answer sheet should have each smelly participant's name and a blank for a number to be filled in.

3 **SMELLY PARTICIPANT DAY:** Give each smelly participant a T-shirt and a mailing envelope. Ask the smelly participants to wear this T-shirt all day, without wearing perfume or anything else with a smell that would help smellers to identify them. Unscented deodorant is okay. When the day is over, have them place the T-shirt in the mailing envelope and bring it to you.

4 **WHEN YOU RECEIVE** the T-shirts, number the envelopes.

IMPORTANT: *Keep a secret list of smelly participants and the numbers of their envelopes.*

5 **SMELLERS DAY:** The next day (before the T-shirts air out too much!) invite your smellers to smell the T-shirts and

try to match them with smelly participants. Give each smeller an answer sheet. Lay the envelopes a short distance apart from one another. Ask smellers to open each envelope, sniff the T-shirt inside, and try to identify the owner by writing the envelope number next to the name on the answer sheet. Make sure each smeller puts his or her name on the answer sheet. Their relationship to each smelly participant is important!

6 **COMPILE YOUR DATA.**

WORKSHOP RESOURCE >>

Yale Medical School's page about the olfactory system:

http://www.med.yale.edu/caim/cnerves/cn1/cn1_1.html

> Note the relationship of each smeller to the smelly participants they successfully identified.

CONSIDER THIS! PRESENT THIS!

> Chart the relationships between smellers and smelly participants. On your chart, use small T-shirt symbols to show how many correct identifications each smeller made.

> GO THE **EXTRA** MILE! Expand this experiment further by including more participants, or consider placing washcloths in the beds of dogs you know. Can you identify your own dog by smelling the washcloth?

LITTLE TADS

(Test whether tadpoles recognize their siblings)

TIME NEEDED >
about two months

SCIENCE > biology

SCIENCE CONCEPTS >
sibling recognition,
shared DNA

ADULT INVOLVEMENT >
Involve an adult in
your decision to raise
tadpoles, from gathering
spawn (eggs) from a
pond, through assisting
in care and feeding, all
the way to releasing
tadpoles or frogs at
the end of the project.
Remember to comply
with all legal guidelines,
including ISEF rules. See
the resources section
for links.

the basics

MOST ANIMALS—INCLUDING people and tadpoles—use smell to identify their mothers, littermates, and yes, spawnmates, focusing on skin, milk, urine, breath, and so on.

the buzz

In an experiment done on toads by S. K. Saidapur and S. Girish at Karnatak University in Dharwad, India, tadpoles hatched from eggs from the same and different ponds were raised in isolation and then reunited. The scientists observed whether they chose to swim near related or unrelated tadpoles.

the lingo

kin—refers to someone you are related to by blood
spawn—a group of fertilized frog eggs

you'll need

frog eggs (see what to do below)
small plastic containers
fishbowls
a fish tank or cooler
fresh water from the pond where you found the eggs, or tap water that has been allowed to sit out for a week to release the chlorine that is in it from the water purification process. Change the water regularly (tip out most of the old water and add new water; this way you don't have to disturb the tadpoles too much).
tadpole food (may include lettuce, bugs, worms, mealworms, pet store frog food)
window screening (a roll of wire mesh with holes too small to allow a tadpole to swim through)
stopwatch or clock or watch with second hand
observation notebook
OPTIONAL: *camera*

> "
> *The ability to **recognize kin by smell** is related to the ability to distinguish self from nonself. Both talents go all the way **back to bacteria.***
> "

— Sara Stein
The Evolution Book (Workman 1986), p. 129

the QUESTION >> Can tadpoles recognize their brothers and sisters?

the PLAN >> Frogs mate and leave their spawn on the surfaces of ponds in the spring. Tadpoles hatched from this spawn can be raised separately, then reunited to test whether they "recognize" their siblings.

NOTE: You can't do this activity with tadpoles or eggs (spawn) ordered through a pet supply company. How will you know if they're from the same spawn or not?

what to do

NOTE: This is a springtime activity. Raising frogs from egg to tadpole can take six weeks or longer. Do it one year for the next year's science fair for maximum success—and brownie points!

1 **LOCATE A FROG** pond. You can sometimes do this by listening for peeper frogs in the spring, or consult a local wildlife center about where frogs might live.

2 **GATHER FROG SPAWN** from three or four locations in the pond, or from different ponds. You'll know you're seeing eggs if the surface of the water seems coated with clear mucus-like scum. Scoop up a small portion and place the eggs in a plastic container. Add some of the pond water. Label clearly: date, time, and location.

3 **TAKE YOUR FROG** eggs home and leave them alone until they hatch. For more on raising tadpoles, check resources.

4 **WHEN THE EGGS** have hatched, you will have tadpoles. You may need to change the water. Gather pond water again from the same pond.

5 **CAREFULLY SCOOP THREE** tadpoles from each container and place each alone in a plastic fishbowl. Continue caring for your tadpoles for a few more days until they seem stronger, older.

6 **PREPARE YOUR FISH** tank or cooler for your experiment by building two screen barriers the width of the tank or cooler. These should be able to stand alone. They should reach from the bottom of the container to the surface of the water, so that tadpoles cannot swim under or over.

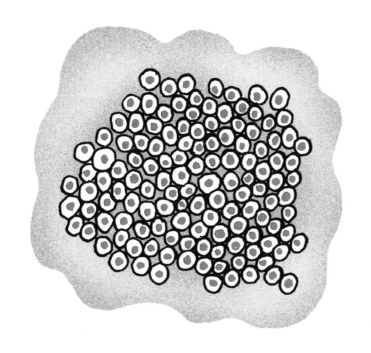

7 **PLACE ONE TADPOLE** from a particular location at one end of the container, confined to that end by the screening. Place a tadpole from another location at the other end.

8 **NOW CHOOSE ANOTHER** tadpole from the same location as one of the tadpoles in the tank. Place it in the water in the middle.

9 **CLOSELY OBSERVE YOUR** middle tadpole to see where it swims; note which end it swims to and whether it stays there or moves away. Use the stopwatch to time the reaction of the tadpole and to see how long it stays at one end or the other.

10 **REPEAT THIS EXPERIMENT** with other combinations of tadpoles to see whether their behavior when given a choice between related tadpoles and unrelated tadpoles follows a pattern.

11 **DOCUMENT YOUR OBSERVATION** with a camera.

WORKSHOP RESOURCES >>

"How to Raise Tadpoles" at the All About Frogs website
http://allaboutfrogs.org/info/tadpoles/

"Raising Tadpoles" at the Missouri Department of Conservation website
http://mdc.mo.gov/conmag/1995/07/60.htm

> Why would it benefit animals to be able to stick with their kin? Why would this ability be useful, or why not?

CONSIDER THIS! PRESENT THIS!

> You can videotape this experiment and show it at your science fair. Write a voice-over, and use iMovie or a program like it to dub your voice in. Make your narrative exciting: Build up the suspense when you put the tadpole into the middle water of the tank. You can even add funny dialogue between the tadpoles being reunited with their long-lost family members.

> GO THE EXTRA MILE! Release your tadpoles back into the ponds they came from, or continue raising your tadpoles until they become frogs, and release them into their home ponds. But do release them, or take them to your local wildlife center.

GOOD CAR, MA
(Test your family car's efficiency)

TIME NEEDED › one to two weeks or more

SCIENCE ›
earth science

SCIENCE CONCEPTS ›
energy use and efficiency

ADULT INVOLVEMENT ›
You'll need the assistance and cooperation of an adult driver.

the basics

YOUR FAMILY car's gas mileage may be affected by a number of factors. You can isolate one factor and see whether you detect a pattern that connects it with your car's mileage. This workshop also shows how you and your sibling(s) may look at several factors to see which appear most closely linked to gas efficiency. Your combined data may show you more than each individual's data.

the buzz

If drivers worldwide can eliminate their use of fossil fuels (including gasoline), we may slow, stop, or reverse climate change. Alternate fuel sources and transportation methods are being explored, but drivers are also trying to reduce their fuel use by driving less and/or finding ways to drive their cars more efficiently.

the lingo

fossil fuels—petroleum-based products like coal, oil, and gasoline are created from the fossilized remains of organisms that lived 300 million years ago and are buried in or under the Earth's crust. When they are burned, they release energy and produce carbon dioxide. Too much carbon dioxide creates an imbalance in the atmosphere that leads to climate change.

you'll need

For all:
notebook
calculator
NOTE: *It helps to do this workshop while studying a regular route, such as your family's daily commute to work and school, or typical around-town driving. You wouldn't want to compare a 50-mile run on flat ground to a 50-mile run in the mountains.*

For air-conditioning experiment:
a car with an air conditioner
NOTE: *This experiment may be done on days with roughly the same outside temperature.*

For tire pressure: access to an air pump; a tire pressure gauge
NOTE: *Ask an expert (at the gas*

the QUESTION >> Does the way we run our car affect its gas mileage?

the PLAN >> Here's a way to get the whole family involved in your science experiment. Measure and compare your car's gas mileage as you change factors of tire pressure, octane, and/ or air-conditioning. If your sibling assesses another factor, and you link to each other's data, your outcomes will be clearer and richer.

station or mechanics' garage) to adjust the tire pressure and measure it for you.

For octane: fuels of two or three different octane levels: regular (87), premium (91), or high octane (93)

what to do

1 **YOU WILL MAKE** three total trips for each experiment. If your siblings choose to study a different factor, they will need to make additional trips.

2 **START WITH** an empty or nearly empty tank and add the same amount of gas each time you pump up. At the start of each trip, record the date, time, amount of gas, and the octane level in your notebook.
NOTE: *It is up to you and your driver how much gas to buy and how far*

to drive. Use the same brand of gas throughout the experiment. For each trip in the experiment, you'll want to drive until your car has gone through the amount of gas you have designated for one trip.

3 **RECORD THE NUMBER** of miles on your car's odometer (on the dashboard, this meter shows the number of total miles your car has driven).

4 **FOR THE AIR** conditioner and tire pressure experiments, change the conditions for each of the three trips:
air conditioner:
a. on
b. off
c. on with windows open

tire pressure: (for example, if your car's safe range is 29 to 34 pounds per square inch [psi])
a. low (29 psi)
b. medium (31.5 psi)
c. high (34 psi)

5 **FOR THE OCTANE** level experiment, fill the gas tank the designated amount per trip with
trip 1: regular gas (87)
trip 2: premium (91)
trip 3: high octane (93)
NOTE: *Check your car's manual to see what fuel the manufacturer recommends. If the manual says not*

to use high octane, experiment with just regular and premium.

6 **DRIVE UNTIL YOUR** car's gas gauge indicates that you have used the amount of gas you decided on. Record the number of miles on the odometer.

7 **TO CALCULATE YOUR** car's gas mileage:

A. Find out how many miles your car drove during this trip. Subtract the first mile number from the second. For example, at the beginning of the trip, your odometer read 60,000 miles. At the end, it reads 60,135. 60,135 — 60,000 = 135 miles.

B. Divide the miles driven by the number of gallons of gas you used. For example, if you used 3 gallons of gas: 135 divided by 3 = 45 miles per gallon (mpg).

8 **REPEAT THE DRIVE** after changing the condition you are measuring.

9 **WHEN YOUR TRIPS** are completed, compare the numbers. Which conditions yielded the best mileage? The worst?

WORKSHOP RESOURCE >>

U.S. Department of Energy fuel economy website
http://www.fueleconomy.gov/

> "
> *Not driving, **driving less,** or driving something else.*
> "
>
> — Car Talk's Guide to Better Fuel Economy

> Based on your findings, do you think your family will change driving habits? Why or why not?

CONSIDER THIS! PRESENT THIS!

> With your siblings, create a website about gas efficiency. Use your page of the site for your demonstration, but also show the links to the data produced by other scientists—your family members.

> GO THE **EXTRA** MILE! Compare your results with those of your siblings. Whose experiment showed the clearest link between conditions and gas mileage?

TRACK A VIRUS
(Study how a cold travels through your class or family)

TIME NEEDED > one to two weeks or more

SCIENCE > microbiology

SCIENCE CONCEPT > transmission of viruses

ADULT INVOLVEMENT > None needed. You may need adult participation, however. Remember to comply with all legal guidelines, including ISEF rules. See the resources section for links.

the basics

THE COMMON cold is a contagious disease caused by a virus, a microorganism that requires a host body to survive. When your body is invaded by a virus, it fights back by trying to push the invader out. The result? Symptoms such as fever, stuffy nose, or sneezing.

the buzz

New cold viruses constantly develop. The symptoms—stuffy nose, cough, sore throat, fever—result from the immune system's efforts to protect the body from the virus. Once you have had a particular cold, you are immune to the virus that caused it, so you won't get it again. Your next cold will come from a virus that is new to your body. Young people get more colds because they have fewer immunities.

the lingo

inoculation—the moment a virus enters your body

latent period—the time between inoculation and the appearance of the first symptom

incubation period—how long after inoculation it takes for an infection (in which the body tries to fight an invader) to develop in response to a virus

index case—subject who serves as the starting point in your study

NOTE: *You can try to prevent catching a cold.*

- Wear a surgical mask.
- Wash your hands frequently with warm water and soap.
- Avoid using your bare hands to take things from someone who has a cold.
- Keep your hands away from your mouth and nose.
- Avoid sharing food and drink.
- Use hand sanitizer.

you'll need

willing subjects at a time when a cold is going around
index cards
sticky notes
blank wall or **bulletin board with tacks**
computer with graphic program or **poster board** and markers

the QUESTION >> What path does a cold virus take to get to—and through—your family?

the PLAN >> Dr. James Crowe, of Vanderbilt-Ingram Cancer Center, who suggested this study, says that the average middle schooler contracts six viruses a year. Gather data from family, friends, classmates, and acquaintances to create a map showing how a virus is transmitted.

> "
> *My identical twin brother and I were both always* **interested in disease,** *but he became a medical doctor and I got a Ph.D. and* **went into research.** *I am trying to understand* **how to prevent people from getting the flu,** *and my brother is trying to understand* **how to care for them if they do get it.**
> "

— Dr. George Hill,
professor of microbiology and immunology, Vanderbilt University

what to do

In advance: Prepare questions for people who get the cold. Make an index card to keep track of information for each person.

1 **SELECT AN INDEX CASE.** Does somebody in your family, class, or community have the cold? Start with this person. This is your *index case.* Make a sticky note with his or her name on it and stick it in the middle of your board or wall.

2 **ASK YOUR INDEX** case person what hurts, what his or her temperature is, how many times per hour he or she coughs, or whatever else he or she feels up to contributing.

3 **REVIEW THE INDEX** case's information. Make sticky notes with the name of each person with the cold that the index case mentions. Get additional information if you can from the index case. For example, if the person says he or she got the cold from his or her family, find out who had the cold first, second, and so on.

4 **GIVE THESE PEOPLE** your questions, and use their answers to add sticky notes representing them to your map. Draw arrows on the map from sticky note to sticky note to show the transmission of the virus.

5 **TRY TO FOLLOW** the cold from each person to the next person who gets it.

6 **CONTINUE QUESTIONING** cold sufferers and mapping them until the cold peters out in your family, class, or community.

7 ANALYZE YOUR DATA.

- Figure out what percentage of the group contracted the cold.
- Find out about those who didn't get the cold. Learn whether they did something else to avoid getting sick (i.e., washed hands, stayed away from sick people, wore a face mask).
- Categorize cold sufferers according to age.
- Compare the initial cold symptom experienced by each person.
- You could compare a seating arrangement in your class with the pattern of cold transmission in the class. Or you could compare a map of your town to see which area had the cold first. Or you could note the placement of people's beds and bedrooms in your house, who shared bathrooms, and/or other activities—for example, comparing a child who stays at home with one who goes to school or comparing the parent who cared for sick people the most to the parent who spent more time out of the home.

WORKSHOP RESOURCE >>

The Centers for Disease Control and Prevention website has information about viruses in your area
http://www.cdc.gov/

Most adults have had numerous viruses, so they are immune to more viruses than are children. For this reason, they may get the virus but have no symptoms or fewer symptoms than children—the difference between a sniffly nose and a running nose, for example.

CONSIDER THIS! PRESENT THIS!

Your map will allow you to draw conclusions about how and why the cold traveled through your group. Show it to public health officials in your area and ask them for their response and input.

GO THE **EXTRA** MILE! Find local statistics on colds during a year. What is the peak month for catching a cold in your area?

NAP MAP

(Identify, map, and compare sleep stages of family members)

TIME NEEDED >
one to two weeks

SCIENCE >
physiology, human behavior

SCIENCE CONCEPT >
sleep study

ADULT INVOLVEMENT >
You'll need permission to observe and/or videotape napping children and/or adults. Remember to comply with all legal guidelines, including ISEF rules. See the resources section for links.

the basics

REM SLEEP is a stage of sleep characterized by rapid eye movement, irregular breathing and heartbeats, and twitches in the hands and feet. During this period, blood flow to the brain increases, and dreams are particularly lively. Sleepwalking and nightmares can happen during REM sleep.

the buzz

REM sleep was first identified in 1952 by scientists who observed it in a small child who seemed to be dreaming. In recent years, sleep labs have become important research centers, where sleep disorders are identified and treated. Electroencephalograms may be used to identify REM and non-REM sleep, but you can identify these stages by watching people, too. Sleep researchers have many different theories on why sleep is important, but they agree that people who don't get enough REM sleep don't function as well or feel as good during their waking hours. To feel healthy, an adult needs about two hours of REM sleep a night. The rest of the six to eight recommended hours of sleep are non-REM sleep.

the lingo

electroencephalogram (EEG)—a graph of brain activity gathered by attaching sensors to the head; a machine "reads" the activity and produces the graph

you'll need

napping people: babies, toddlers, children of different ages, adults, senior citizens
a watch or clock
OPTIONAL: video camera

the QUESTION >> Can you observe the stages of sleep? How do people of different ages compare in REM patterns?

the PLAN >> Observe family members of different ages as they sleep, identify their REM stages, and compare the percentage of their sleep that the REM stages take up.

NOTE: It's up to you to determine what range of ages and people you observe. You may choose to observe and compare all your family members or compare several children of approximately the same age. You might consider including the family dog in this study as an interesting comparison. Dogs have REM sleep, too!

what to do

1 PRACTICE OBSERVING and identifying rapid eye movement (REM). Ask a friend or family member to close his or her eyes, and, with eyes closed, move his or her eyes around as though looking left, right, up, and down. This is how REM may look in sleep, but the eyes may move more rapidly under the eyelids.

2 ASK THE PARENT of the baby or toddler you're going to observe how long a typical nap is. Overall, try not to interfere too much with the length of someone's natural nap. Your data will involve percentage of the nap time taken up by REM sleep, so having everybody sleep the same length of time isn't that important.

3 SETTLE YOURSELF QUIETLY with your watch or clock near your subject as he or she tries to fall asleep. Observe the length of time and activities (turning, etc.) before you're sure the subject is "out." Continue observing movements, jotting down the time things take place and noting the changes, including REM sleep.

OPTIONAL: *Videotape one or more subjects during sleep.*

4 WHEN THE NAP is done, use your data to map it in minutes and calculate the percentage of time spent in REM phases.

5 REPEAT YOUR NAP watch with other subjects, then compare the results of your observations. What generalizations can you draw from your data? How do the graphs vary?

WORKSHOP RESOURCE >>

Neuroscience for Kids, Univ. of Washington, sleep section
http://faculty.washington.edu/chudler/sleep.html

> Why would a person of a different age need a different amount of sleep, or different amounts of a different kind of sleep? How could you confirm your theory about this? What further study would be needed?

CONSIDER THIS! PRESENT THIS!

> Make a stop-action animation of your line graph. Make your line graph on your computer, or draw it by hand and scan the drawings in. Draw it at four to six different time points, making the line extend further each time. Then import your drawings into a slideshow such as iPhoto. As your pictures play, the line will seem to grow. You can also add a sound track of different music to demonstrate the change from REM to non-REM sleep.

> GO THE **EXTRA** MILE! Experiment with getting an hour extra sleep every day for a week. Study yourself. Does the additional sleep make a difference?

PRESENT IT!

Handing It In, Showing It Off, Telling Your Story, Getting the "A"

HERE IS a list of things you'll definitely want to include in your table display and report for your science fair. For more, see the workshops, especially Present This! and Go the Extra Mile!

INCLUDE IT!

Include your starting question(s), procedures, tools, data (facts), findings (results), notes, conclusion (decision based on the facts and results), and a follow-up question. Provide a listing of your research: articles, books, websites, interviews, and other information sources you used.

DRAW IT!

You're working with visible objects. Learn all you can about them by looking, and then communicate it through artwork. Include all the parts of the situation you are investigating.

GRAPH IT!

Computer graphics programs make it easy to put your data into graph form. Check out these websites for making graphs:

- Statistics Canada http://www.statcan.gc.ca/edu/power-pouvoir/ch9/picto-figuratifs/5214825-eng.htm
- National Center for Education Statistics www.nces.ed.gov/nceskids/graphing/classic/

POWERPOINT IT!

Use a computer to coordinate your graphs, photographs, videos, and other materials into a presentation. You can set up your PowerPoint to loop continually, present it to your teacher on a DVD, and add it to your school portfolio.

NOTE: *The Macintosh program Keynote is similar to PowerPoint.*

DRAMATIZE IT!

Consider the impact of recordings, dramatic performances, costumes, posters, sound effects, and more! There's plenty of room for creativity and drama in science.

PHOTOGRAPH IT!

- **Still photography**
- **Animation**—Use still shots to make a stop-action movie. Take four to six shots, then use a computer program such as iMovie to make the stills flash by like a flip book, so your viewer sees movement and change.
- **Time lapse**—Set up a still camera or video camera to take an image every 30 seconds. The result will be a series of still shots that seem to move and morph over time.
- **Video**
- **Flexi-cam** is a camera with a magnifying lens, attached to a TV or computer. Viewers can see a tadpole or other things that are alive and in motion, as well as things that aren't. Track down a flexi-cam in your school's science lab or media room, or see if a local university has one you can borrow.

the resources

The International Science and Engineering Fair rules are here: http://www.societyforscience.org/Page.aspx?pid=312
All research involving humans and vertebrate animals in any facility, including schools, universities, labs, and for science fairs, requires prior approval and is subject to strict guidelines. You can find more information at these two links: http://ethics.ucsd.edu/courses/integrity/assignments/animal.html and http://www.hhs.gov/ohrp/irb/irb_guidebook.htm

SCIENCE SUPPLIES
Science Stuff, www.sciencestuff.com
Science Company, www.sciencecompany.com
Basic Science Supplies, www.basicsciencesupplies.com

BOOKS
Oh, Brother... Oh, Sister! A Sister's Guide to Getting Along by Brooks Whitney (American Girl 2008).

Born to Rebel: Birth Order, Family Dynamics, and Creative Lives by Frank J. Sulloway (Pantheon 1996).

Sibshops: Workshops for Siblings of Children with Special Needs by Donald J. Meyer and Patricia F. Vadasy (Paul H. Brookes 2007).

Entwined Lives: Twins and What They Tell Us About Human Behavior by Nancy L. Segal (Dutton 1999).

Indivisible by Two: Lives of Extraordinary Twins by Nancy L. Segal (Harvard University Press 2007).

WEBSITES
Learn Genetics: Genetic Science Learning Center, University of Utah http://learn.genetics.utah.edu/

Science Buddies www.sciencebuddies.com

DNA From the Beginning (science concepts and animations) http://www.dnaftb.org/dnaftb/1/concept/index.html

U.S. Department of Agriculture, National Institute of Food and Agriculture page on Family Science: http://www.csrees.usda.gov/familyscience.cfm
Twins Today (iParenting Media) http://www.twinstoday.com

index